WALK THR

rest

40 DAYS OF REFRESHMENT FOR WOMEN

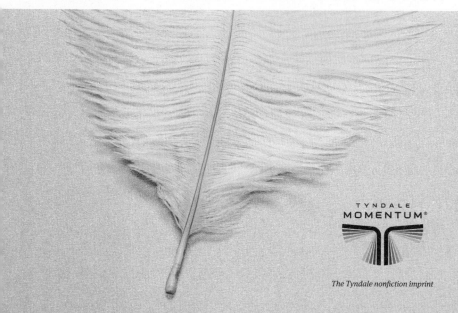

TYNDALE
MOMENTUM®

The Tyndale nonfiction imprint

Visit Tyndale online at tyndale.com.

Visit Tyndale Momentum online at tyndalemomentum.com.

TYNDALE, Tyndale's quill logo, *Tyndale Momentum*, and the Tyndale Momentum logo are registered trademarks of Tyndale House Ministries. Tyndale Momentum is the nonfiction imprint of Tyndale House Publishers, Carol Stream, Illinois.

Walk Thru the Bible and the Walk Thru the Bible logo are registered trademarks of Walk Thru the Bible Ministries, Inc.

Rest: 40 Days of Refreshment for Women

Copyright © 2021 by Walk Thru the Bible. All rights reserved.

Some of the devotions were previously published by Walk Thru the Bible in *Journey* magazine and have been adapted from *The One Year Daily Moments of Peace*.

Cover photograph of ostrich feather copyright © MirageC/Getty Images. All rights reserved.

Designed by Dean H. Renninger and Julie Chen

Unless otherwise indicated, all Scripture quotations are taken from the *Holy Bible*, New Living Translation, copyright © 1996, 2004, 2015 by Tyndale House Foundation. Used by permission of Tyndale House Publishers, Carol Stream, Illinois 60188. All rights reserved.

Scripture quotations marked ESV are from The ESV® Bible (The Holy Bible, English Standard Version®), copyright © 2001 by Crossway, a publishing ministry of Good News Publishers. Used by permission. All rights reserved.

Scripture quotations marked HCSB are taken from the Holman Christian Standard Bible,® copyright © 1999, 2000, 2002, 2003, 2009 by Holman Bible Publishers. Used by permission. Holman Christian Standard Bible,® Holman CSB,® and HCSB® are federally registered trademarks of Holman Bible Publishers.

Scripture quotations marked KJV are taken from the *Holy Bible*, King James Version.

Scripture quotations marked NASB are taken from the New American Standard Bible,® copyright © 1960, 1962, 1963, 1968, 1971, 1972, 1973, 1975, 1977, 1995 by The Lockman Foundation. Used by permission.

Scripture quotations marked NIV are taken from the Holy Bible, *New International Version*,® *NIV*.® Copyright © 1973, 1978, 1984, 2011 by Biblica, Inc.® Used by permission. All rights reserved worldwide.

For information about special discounts for bulk purchases, please contact Tyndale House Publishers at csresponse@tyndale.com, or call 1-800-323-9400.

ISBN 978-1-4964-5083-8

Printed in the United States of America

27	26	25	24	23	22	21
7	6	5	4	3	2	1

Introduction

Rest often feels like an elusive goal in a world that never seems to shut down—or even slow down. Given all the demands on your time, energy, and resources, does your longing for calm, quiet, and stillness ever seem unrealistic or selfish?

If so, Scripture reveals something surprising. The only source of true peace and refreshment, it shows us, is God Himself. After the disciples returned from their first ministry tour, they excitedly told Jesus everything they'd seen and done. Given how much work remained, did Jesus send them right back out into the neighboring towns? No. Instead, He told them, "Let's go off by ourselves to a quiet place and rest awhile" (Mark 6:31).

Likewise, this book is an invitation for you to spend a few minutes each day in quiet contemplation, whether it be first thing in the morning, over your lunch break, or just before bed. God made you and me to function best (and be most at peace) when we regularly take time to connect with Him through Scripture and prayer. As God told the

Israelites, "Only in returning to me and resting in me will you be saved. In quietness and confidence is your strength" (Isaiah 30:15).

Rest can be your means of connecting with God for a few moments a day. These devotions are written by women from all walks of life whose stories will encourage you to embrace the peace and refreshment that is yours when you remember and rest in God's goodness, power, and love for you.

Each reading ends with a prayer to help you begin a longer conversation with God about the people and situations He has put on your heart. If you'd like to go deeper with that day's topic, be sure to turn to the Scripture passage referenced in the Rest in Him section.

This book is an invitation for you to hear and meditate on God's Word as you relax, recharge, and reconnect with Christ, the one who "himself is our peace" (Ephesians 2:14, esv).

A Quiet Sanctuary

Search for the LORD and for his strength;
continually seek him.

1 CHRONICLES 16:11

One Sunday afternoon I headed out for a walk through a nearby forest preserve. As I started out on the limestone trail that circles the lake, I felt my body relax. My mind and heart, which had been on overdrive all week, felt lighter. In this place of calm, I began to pray silently as I watched prairie grasses bend and sway gently in the breeze. Tiny waves lapped the rocky shore. When I passed an inlet, I stopped to listen to a chorus of birds chirping from a small stand of trees growing along the water's edge.

Suddenly a rumble from above interrupted the symphony. I watched as a plane zoomed overhead, its engines drowning out the birdsong. No sooner had its sound faded than another plane emerged from the clouds, filling the air with a familiar rumble. Just twenty-five miles from Chicago's O'Hare Airport, the forest preserve was clearly in one of its flight paths.

Just minutes before, talking with God had seemed easy as I poured out my concerns and sensed Him bringing encouraging Scriptures to mind. Now I simply wanted to finish walking the loop around the lake and head home.

When I got to thinking about how my prayer time was cut short that afternoon, I realized it wasn't all that different from my experience when starting the day with prayer. I am easily distracted. If it's not the hum of a plane engine, it's the sudden thought of a phone call I need to return or the memory of an argument with my husband. Worse, if I don't guard my heart, my prayers can devolve into a laundry list of worries.

Like those approaching planes, my anxious thoughts so easily break the calm sanctuary the Spirit longs to establish in me. However, while I can't alter a plane's flight path, Scripture tells me I can redirect my disruptive musings. I can confess and turn my worries over to the Holy Spirit. I can pray Scripture passages that relate to a concern I have for a family member, knowing God will always fulfill His promises.

Christ is still the Good Shepherd who "lets me rest in green meadows" and who "leads me beside peaceful streams" (Psalm 23:2)—even when I'm not in a secluded (or noise-free) forest preserve.

Rest Assured

Heavenly Father, when distractions and noise threaten to drown out Your voice today, draw me close and remind me of Your unfailing promises and love for me.

Rest in Him: 2 Corinthians 1:20-22

words of reflection

Nor Does He Sleep

He holds all creation together.
COLOSSIANS 1:17

She was sitting in her car seat, singing at the top of her lungs: "He is exhausted, the King is exhausted on high, I will praise Him. . . . He is the Rord . . ."

We were on our way home from church that Sunday afternoon and had just sung that song in the service. Of course, our daughter had a few of the words wrong (exchange *exalted* for *exhausted*, and *Lord* for *Rord*).

But her rendition of the song got me thinking. Who would blame God for being exhausted? Just listening to my own prayers would make an ordinary person tired. And He listens to the tiniest prayers of His children all over the world. Just taking care of and providing for my little family is a full-time job. But He takes care of and provides for everyone.

He causes His rain to fall on the evil and the good. He sees everything—all the good deeds and all the sin. He holds the universe in place, and He knits our bodies together. He calls the stars out by name every night, and He gives me every breath I take. He had a plan of salvation for the world from the very beginning, and He has a plan for my four-year-old daughter's life.

What if He decided to chuck it all and take a nap? What if He said, "Whew. I've had enough. These people are wearing Me out. I need a break"?

Scripture tells us "he holds all creation together" (Colossians 1:17)—that means every cell in our bodies and this planet that we live on. It means that every single creature and every single human being depend on Him for survival. And it also means that He knows your name and what each day of your life is going to look like.

Remember, God is never asleep at the wheel. He's in charge of all that's going on around the globe, and He never takes a day off.

Rest in the truth that God is fully aware of all that is going on in your life. He is tireless in His pursuit, protection, and provision for you.

Rest Assured

Father, thank You that You will never leave us or forsake us. We can relax in the knowledge that You are sovereign over all things, even our very next breath.

Rest in Him: Colossians 1:15-20

words of reflection

When Answers Don't Come

*All of God's promises have been fulfilled in Christ
with a resounding "Yes!"*

2 CORINTHIANS 1:20

Tears filled Gayla's eyes as the leader of her prayer group spoke of her daughter's years of rebellion. Ten years passed before God drew her back and restored her to their family. The leader's final comment struck hard. She said, "I have discovered that God doesn't always tell us yes or no when we pray. But sometimes He says, 'I have a better plan.'"

Gayla pondered those words as she considered her own circumstances. Her family had had its share of problems over the last year, causing division and angst in their household. She'd asked God to restore her family, but it hadn't happened. God seemed unresponsive to their circumstances, and she'd begun to lose hope.

God, Gayla prayed, *forgive me for not trusting Your goodness and believing that You still hear me, love me, and have a better plan. Thank You for all the ways You sustain and carry me. Help me to be faithful as I wait for You to accomplish Your work in our lives.*

Sometimes our lives seem to be littered with "unanswered prayers"—the healing that didn't happen, unreconciled relationships, the home that was foreclosed, the great job that eludes us. Even in those times of waiting or closed doors, we can know God has a better plan because we know His character. He is good, wise, loving, merciful, and compassionate. He is the One who has "a future and a hope" for us (Jeremiah 29:11). His plan is to develop in us the character of Christ and draw us near to Him, however He chooses to do that.

There are times in our lives when we must determine to bow before Him in surrender and run to Romans 11:33, which declares, "Oh, how great are God's riches and wisdom and knowledge! How impossible it is for us to understand his decisions and his ways!"

Rest Assured

Father, help my unbelief. Give me the faith to trust You even when the answers don't seem to make sense.

Rest in Him: Psalm 86

words of reflection

In the Details

Your Father knows exactly what you need even before you ask him!
MATTHEW 6:8

Recently I found myself walking briskly through the airport, trying to work off some nervous energy. As much as I enjoy traveling, I'd taken this long nonstop flight before and knew it to be a stressful experience. In the hours leading up to it, I'd mentally prepared myself to navigate one of the world's busiest airports and endure a long-haul flight alone.

I wonder how experienced the pilot is, I'd thought hours earlier. *I hope he's competent.*

That thought was still in the back of my mind when I reached my gate and learned that the plane was running late. Joining the crowd in the waiting area, I plopped myself down and struck up a conversation with the uniformed flight attendant beside me.

One by one, other crew members arrived and came over to where we were seated until the entire flight crew, pilot and copilot included, had joined the conversation. They were happy to tell me about their line of work, and since I was well acquainted with our destination, I answered their questions about the area. As the pilot took coffee orders for the crew and insisted I add mine to the list, I thought back sheepishly to my earlier cynicism.

So began the best commercial flight I've ever been on. Other passengers regarded me with growing curiosity as the crew greeted me by name and kept a friendly eye out for me over the hours. Technically, I traveled alone that day, but in reality, I had company nearly from the moment I cleared security until deplaning.

Sometimes it's easy to see God in life's dramatic moments, when the stakes are high and the impossible looms. But He is no less real or evident in the little things. My travel concerns, while not earth-shattering, still weighed on my heart, but God already had the details worked out in a way that surpassed what I could have come up with. Isn't that just like God, to take such an interest in our lives and leave His fingerprints in the details? Only He could orchestrate that level of detail, using the nuance of each moment to show His care and control.

Rest Assured

Thank You, Father, for the way You show Yourself in the details, knowing and arranging circumstances long before they even cross my mind!

Rest in Him: Psalm 8

words of reflection

Knowing His Will

For the LORD grants wisdom!
From his mouth come knowledge and understanding.

Leah attempted to stifle the familiar feeling of anxiety threat-ening to overtake her. She longed to be obedient to God, but sometimes it seemed truly difficult to know His will. She wrestled with so many decisions, and she knew this anxiety could not be His intention for her. Now she had been offered an exciting ministry position requiring increased responsi-bility and an extra time commitment.

"Oh, God," she cried out, "how can I know what Your will is for me regarding this?" Even as she prayed, she recalled a discussion with her friend Bonnie about seeking God's will.

Bonnie had said, "First I read Scripture and then I pray, asking God to speak and help me hear. Then I ask godly friends for counsel. I see how the opportunity fits with my passion and gifts. I also remember God often calls me to work that requires His power to keep me dependent on Him. I then ask Him to confirm what I'm thinking and hearing."

Leah remembered the words from Psalm 94:19: "When

my anxious thoughts multiply within me, Your consolations delight my soul" (NASB). She relaxed, knowing God would show her what she needed to see.

Today's culture offers a multitude of choices. Our lives are bombarded with decisions, from what to eat, wear, and drive, to where we'll live and work, to whom we'll marry. We could become immobilized just anticipating choices and their outcomes. For Christians wanting to serve and please God, making these decisions can be especially difficult. But remember that we serve a God who "is a wonderful teacher" and who gives "great wisdom" (Isaiah 28:29). We can turn to Him through Bible reading and prayer, and He will direct our paths.

Rest Assured

Father, You are my Wonderful Counselor. Thank You that You will direct my path and order my steps for Your purposes.

Rest in Him: Proverbs 2:1-6

words of reflection

DAY 6

Sabbath Rest

Observe the Sabbath day by keeping it holy, as the LORD your God has commanded you. You have six days each week for your ordinary work, but the seventh day is a Sabbath day of rest dedicated to the LORD your God.

DEUTERONOMY 5:12-14

When my children were little, I looked forward to a simple Sunday afternoon ritual all week long. After church and a lunch of grilled cheese or PB and J, my husband would put the kids down for a nap, and I'd head to the local bookstore.

As soon as I walked through the heavy wooden doors, I was met with the sweet, rich smell of paper and coffee. After browsing a bit, perhaps picking up a book or magazine I might want to buy, I'd order a latte and settle myself at one of the café tables. After spending some time digging into my bookstore finds, I'd get out my weekly journal and jot down answers to a few questions: "What went well this week?" "What should I try differently next week?" and "What did God teach me this week?" My musings weren't life changing, but they did help me decide what was effective and what wasn't in my busy schedule as a working mom, as well as reminding me of the ways God had shown up in my life over the past seven days.

Celebrating the Sabbath, I've come to believe, doesn't mean just going to church. It is an invitation from God to sit with Him and tarry a bit so that He can speak to our hearts and recharge our bodies. At other seasons in my life, I've done that by taking a walk around my neighborhood, soaking in a bathtub, or even trying out a new soup recipe. The setting is less important than acknowledging my need for rest, purposefully stepping away from unfinished chores, and opening my heart to God's still, small voice.

Rest Assured

Father, thank You for designing the Sabbath so that my body gets the rest it needs and my soul has time to rest in You.

Rest in Him: Mark 2:23-27

words of reflection

Pursuing Passion

*You must love the LORD your God with all your heart, all your soul,
all your mind, and all your strength.*

MARK 12:30

Carole's mind was anywhere but in her Bible study class. She
was racing through her mental to-do list, wondering how it
could possibly get done and thinking perhaps she shouldn't
have even taken the time to attend today. But the voice of
Kim, her study leader, finally broke through.

"The Bible clearly teaches that God is to be our primary
passion—we are to love Him with all our heart, soul, mind,
and strength. We are to have no idols. Most of us believe we
do put God first and certainly serve no idols. But is this really
so? Is He really our primary passion?"

Carole began shifting uncomfortably as Kim continued.

"Christian women today can easily get caught up in our
to-do lists and the demands of life and lose our focus. We
can misplace our true passion by trying to please others or
chasing affirmation. Perhaps we need to consider what regularly receives the bulk of our time, attention, and resources.
If we discover God's percentage of our affection is actually

small, we need to make the choice to return to our first love. Remember, you can trust God to faithfully direct your path when you 'seek his will in all you do'" (Proverbs 3:6).

Oh Father, Carole silently prayed, *forgive me for being so distracted. Please restore my passion for You.*

What would misplaced passion look like? It could be revealed by a strong attraction to the culture. It could be reflected in a great concern for physical beauty, a materialistic focus, a loss of hunger for God's Word, and a diminished heart for His kingdom work. It might look like apathy or perhaps a lack of loyalty to the body of Christ, His church.

God is glad to do a heart check if we ask Him. He rejoices to see His children make a fresh surrender to His plans for us.

Rest Assured

Your loving-kindness, grace, and mercy toward me are without limits, Lord. Help me daily to renew my commitment to seek Your glory and walk in Your ways.

Rest in Him: Colossians 3:1-4

words of reflection

How Can I Repay?

*God saved you by his grace when you believed. And you can't
take credit for this; it is a gift from God.*

EPHESIANS 2:8

Jodi opened the door to Frances, who stepped around the
toys littering the entryway. Bouncing one baby on her hip,
Jodi closed the door before the other baby could crawl out.

"You certainly have your hands full now that these two
are crawling," commented Frances. She clapped her hands
playfully and reached for the baby in Jodi's arms.

The baby easily left her mother's embrace and grabbed
hold of Frances. Meanwhile, Jodi lifted her teetering son into
her arms and beckoned Frances to follow her.

"Frances, you've done so much for me," Jodi began. "Are
you sure you want to take the twins again today?"

"I remember what it was like as a young mom," Frances
replied. "And I had a mom living close by who helped out.
You don't have that. Besides, I love taking the babies for a
stroll around the park."

Jodi gathered things into the diaper bag, but she felt the
familiar guilt surfacing as she prepared to send her babies

off with Frances for the afternoon. How could she ever repay her? The older woman must have sensed Jodi's hesitance because she put down the baby and wrapped her arms around the young mom.

"Jodi," she whispered, "I know how hard your days can be, and I just want to show you a little grace. God has blessed me with time and energy to spare. It's my pleasure to share it with you."

Grace is given with enthusiasm, goodwill, and no strings attached. The gracious giver has an abundance to offer, and the recipient stands in humble need with no way to repay. Have you ever been the recipient of such grace? You have if you've come to Jesus, broken and desperate for forgiveness and mercy. To our great relief, God, who is rich in every resource, graciously gives love, mercy, restoration, peace, and more. Praise your gracious God today. You cannot repay Him, but you can sing His praises.

Rest Assured

Father, thank You for graciously giving me all I need for life. Thank You for fresh starts, new hope, and abundant joy, all gifts of amazing grace!

Rest in Him: Ephesians 2:1-10

words of reflection

Perfect Peace

I am leaving you with a gift—peace of mind and heart.
And the peace I give is a gift the world cannot give.
So don't be troubled or afraid.

JOHN 14:27

As Mary drove to the hospital, she fought the urge to fear the worst. She'd received a call from her husband's boss saying that there had been an accident. Mary's frantic mind began to fill in the missing pieces. Perhaps Jack had fallen from the scaffolding on the building he was examining. Perhaps he'd experienced a heart attack. Or maybe he'd been in a car accident between job sites.

But as Mary drove past a small church nestled beneath a grove of trees, she noticed a simple sign in the parking lot. It read, "His peace trumps your understanding." Mary read the words aloud and then remembered a corresponding Scripture in Philippians 4:7. She recited the familiar verse to herself several times as she drove on. When she parked her car at the hospital, Mary felt God giving her the peace He promised.

Lord, I don't know what I'm about to walk into, but You do, Mary prayed. *I will simply trust You. Please guard my heart with Your peace so I can handle whatever lies ahead.*

It's easy to have peace when we feel we have everything under control, when all is going smoothly. But when we can't see what lies ahead or when we don't know all the details of our current struggle, things become more unnerving. And when our problems seem out of our control or the crisis is intensifying, it's easy to lose our calm.

But God promises that those who keep their minds focused and dependent on Him will have perfect peace. While we may think we need all the facts and background information, God just asks us to trust Him with the details. He can give peace that is better than any measure of our own understanding.

What dilemma have you been trying to solve? What fear have you been wrestling? No matter what it is, trust Him, and He will give you peace that surpasses all understanding.

Rest Assured

Father, sometimes I want more information, more control, or more input. But I know that what I really need is to trust You so I can have peace.

Rest in Him: Philippians 4:4-9

words of reflection

The Gain of Giving

God bought you with a high price.
So you must honor God with your body.

1 CORINTHIANS 6:20

Ellen sat across from her college roommate in a booth at a local coffee shop, catching up about Mandy's mission trip to Guatemala.

"When I gave up my spring break to go to Guatemala, I had no idea that I would actually feel more refreshed at the end of the week than I would have if I'd gone to the beach," said Mandy.

"Well, you certainly look great," Ellen replied. "But I thought you were doing physical labor, digging for water and such. Aren't you exhausted?"

Mandy chuckled. "Well, we actually used machinery to 'dig' for the water, but, yes, it was hard work. When I wasn't involved in digging the well, I was playing with the children or walking with the women to the closest water source. So truthfully, it was an exhausting week."

Ellen looked pensively at her friend as she continued sharing. Ellen had been sensing God's call to serve a two-year missionary term after graduating college but had wondered if postponing graduate school that long would be wise. After hearing Mandy's report on her short-term mission trip, Ellen felt confirmation that the price of putting off grad school would be minimal compared to the eternal impact of obeying God's call.

"I thought I was making such a sacrifice," Mandy said as the two gathered their things to leave, "but in the end I gained more than I gave."

True sacrifice doesn't consist of self-deprivation for no purpose. Jesus showed us through His death on the cross that sacrifice costs a great deal but ultimately yields something of great value. Jesus' death, a painful and humiliating price paid by the One who owed absolutely nothing, achieved for us peace with God and eternal life.

If God is asking you to make a sacrifice for His Kingdom, you can know for certain that He will bring great gain from the price you pay.

Rest Assured

Father, I can't always see the benefit of the sacrifice You call me to, but I can trust You to bring good from it in the end.

Rest in Him: Philippians 2:1-11

words of reflection

The Guide

*Lead me by your truth and teach me, for you are the God
who saves me. All day long I put my hope in you.*

PSALM 25:5

When we married twenty years ago, Don and I went to
Europe for our honeymoon. Our trip coincided with a visit
to his company's headquarters in Switzerland.

We decided to map out our own trip, rent a car, and drive
through the countryside, stopping at little inns along the
way. No planned group trip for us!

When we landed in Frankfurt, I was immediately struck
by every difference. The air smelled different. The cus-
toms were different. The language, food, money, and street
layouts—all different.

We learned the hard way that if you didn't get your money
converted at a bank before Friday's closing time, you were
without cash for the weekend (this *was* twenty years ago).
Some places wouldn't take a credit card, and no amount of
pleading and flashing of the plastic could gain us access to a
cash-only inn.

When ordering at a restaurant, we could only point at

menu items hoping they were something we would want to eat. Loud talking and pantomimes didn't help anyone understand us. We vowed to learn to speak German and French fluently as soon as we got home.

We also got hopelessly lost a few times. No amount of logic or intellect could help us figure out the street layouts. I actually said to my husband, "We're lost! Our families will never see us again!"

We needed a guide. And in our daily lives, here on earth, we need the Guide. Our earthly currency of sin and selfishness will never gain us entry into God's Kingdom. Our logic can't help us become more Christlike. Our language of busyness and materialism is not the King's language of love and sacrifice.

Listen to God, our everlasting Guide. He is trustworthy and true, and you'll never lose your way. Depend on Jesus— our source of salvation is also our road map. He will help us navigate the confusing paths of this life until we are safely home with Him.

Rest Assured

Lord, thank You for guiding us through this life to live with You forever.

Rest in Him: Isaiah 58:8-12

words of reflection

Heart of Worry

Worry weighs a person down.

PROVERBS 12:25

I feel like a little kid, I thought to myself. *It's just a trip to the dentist.* I was very nervous about my dental checkup, mostly because I suspected I had a cavity. No one likes pain, and my checking account couldn't take a big hit either. I was tempted to fret and fear and even cancel the appointment. But that would just be avoiding the issue and risking my tooth getting even worse.

Lord, I am so anxious right now, I prayed in the waiting room. *You tell me that I'm not supposed to worry about anything, and that everything will be used for my good and Your glory. Please help me look at this from Your perspective. Remind me that You are with me and You will take care of me.*

Sure enough, I did have a cavity. But I tried to have a good attitude—I didn't complain about the cost, and I went the extra mile to be kind to the dental staff who were caring for me. Only God knows how He will use a little trial like a cavity in the grand scheme of things, but I do know that He calls me to be obedient in the little things—including not worrying about the details of life.

Worry is one of those things that we're tempted to downplay because it doesn't seem to hurt anyone or cause any trouble. Yet Jesus died for all our sins—including worry. When it surfaces, ask God to replace your fear with a deep, abiding trust in Him. Meditate on Scriptures that address your worry triggers, and live in the peace of knowing that our good, wise, infinite God loves you and cares for you. He is with you during difficult times when things may look hopeless.

Rest Assured

Lord, calm my fears and help me live in the truth of Your promises and Your presence.

Rest in Him: Psalm 13

words of reflection

DAY 13

He Is with Us

Here on earth you will have many trials and sorrows.

JOHN 16:33

Heather was a brand-new Christian, and she was excited about Jesus. She had just begun reading the Bible, and I was privileged to mentor her. One morning she stopped by after dropping off her kids at school. Before I had a chance to turn off the TV in the family room, she noticed a news clip about a devastating earthquake in another country. People were still looking for survivors in the rubble.

"How awful. I'm sure glad we won't have to suffer like that," Heather said.

"What do you mean?" I asked.

"Well, we're Christians. God doesn't want us to suffer."

"Heather, God doesn't enjoy seeing us go through hard times, but Jesus does say that we will have suffering in this world."

"Really? If God is good and He loves us, why would He allow us to suffer?" she asked.

"When Adam and Eve sinned in the Garden of Eden by

39

disobeying God, that changed things," I said. "Now we live in a fallen world, and sin, death, violence, natural disasters, wars, and disease are all part of it. Just because we're Christians doesn't mean we're immune to suffering. But in spite of all the things we may have to go through in our lives, God loves us and promises to be with us in the midst of our pain."

Some people have the mistaken impression that Christians don't have to go through difficult times. Especially in the United States, where we have so much, it can be hard to imagine the living conditions among the poorest of the poor. We don't like to think about the fact that tens of thousands of people die every day from hunger or that natural disasters can affect countless people.

But God has promised to be there with us. Isaiah 43:2 says, "When you go through deep waters, I will be with you. When you go through rivers of difficulty, you will not drown."

Rest Assured

God, You are my "refuge and strength, always ready to help in times of trouble." Therefore, I will not be afraid (Psalm 46:1-2).

Rest in Him: John 16:25-33

words of reflection

Put It to Rest

When doubts filled my mind, your comfort
gave me renewed hope and cheer.

PSALM 94:19

Katie gently turned onto her back. She didn't want to wake John, but she didn't want to get up. She just wanted to go back to sleep. She had been awake since 2:00 a.m., and her mind was racing. For the past hour Katie had wrestled with one worrisome thought after another. Even the smallest problems seemed to loom large in her mind during the middle of the night. She felt the urge to get up and set things right, make some necessary phone calls, balance the checkbook, and check out some information on the Internet. She recognized all of these as irrational thoughts. Still, they fired through her mind rapidly, one anxious thought after another.

Finally Katie remembered some advice she'd heard recently on a Christian radio show. The guest had talked about how Satan uses a tired and unguarded mind to set up land mines of anxiety. Katie recognized that her mind was like an exploding minefield, and she needed to follow the advice given.

Katie tried to relax her body by concentrating on her breathing. Then she began to meditate on God's character by going through the alphabet and naming one attribute of God after another: almighty, beautiful, counselor, deliverer, eternal. Dwelling on Him and resisting the urge to worry about other things, Katie finally drifted back to sleep. Her anxious thoughts had been put to rest.

The Bible says not to be anxious about anything, but to handle all our concerns with prayer. But when anxious thoughts multiply rapidly, it can be a challenge to get our minds calm enough to pray. If anxiety has been robbing you of peace often, it might be wise to consult a Christian counselor. And we all need to learn to recognize anxious thoughts so we can counteract them with truth and sound thinking.

Rest Assured

Father, I don't want anxiety to rob me of Your peace. Help me guard my mind against anxious thoughts.

Rest in Him: Psalm 4

words of reflection

The Widow's Might

*There came a certain poor widow,
and she threw in two mites, which make a farthing.*

MARK 12:42, KJV

She came into the Temple complex, the lowest of the low (a woman *and* a widow), the poorest of the poor. She made her way to the treasury, which was a trumpet-shaped metal offering box. She waited in line to make her gift as others with more money made a show of giving it.

Then she threw in two tiny coins, which were worth very little. Certainly not enough to make a difference to anyone.

She turned away, facing an evening with not much to eat.

But the Master was watching her. He saw what she did. And He knew—He knew that she was poor, that she was a widow, that she gave everything she had. And He talked to the disciples about all the people who had more wealth and were making large gifts. In God's math, Jesus tells us, the widow gave more than any of them because she gave out of her poverty; they gave out of their wealth. She held nothing back; they still had plenty.

I wonder: When I give, do I hold back? Do I give because

I have to? Is it a duty or a privilege? An act of obligation or an act of worship? When I serve, do I look for fanfare? Do I pick the glamour jobs? Am I just as happy to change a diaper as I am to serve on the deacon-nominating committee? Do I serve out of gratitude for the Giver? When I share my talents and do what God made me to do, is it about me? Or is it about the One who gave me those talents? Am I noisy with a "look-at-me" attitude, or do I go about quietly, humbly?

I like to think that Jesus provided miraculously for this widow—that someone invited her to dinner that night, or gave her a sack of barley or a jar of oil. We're not told what happened to her, but this brief moment of her life was noticed and recorded for eternity for us to read. She dared to love God, dared to have faith that He would provide, dared to give all. May I do no less.

Rest Assured

Father, thank You for the truths You share with us in Scripture. Thank You for noticing even the smallest acts of faith and love.

Rest in Him: Mark 12:41-44

words of reflection

Reading Ahead

And the one sitting on the throne said,
"Look, I am making everything new!"

REVELATION 21:5

I love to read—books, magazines, articles on the Internet, whatever. I come from a long line of readers; I like to think it's in my genetic makeup.

I was talking recently with another book lover, and I confessed to the habit of reading ahead at times. My friend laughed and said he couldn't believe I would do that. But when the story's action gets intense or the leading character looks like she might not make it or even if I get bored, I turn to the last few pages of the book. By knowing the end of the story, I can relax and read the rest of the book at a slower pace. That way, I don't miss important details, and I'm not skimming because I'm anxious to know what's going to happen. Also, by knowing the end of the story, I can decide if it's worth the time to keep reading.

Isn't it that way in our lives, too? Sometimes when our stories look scary, we want to close the book out of fear. We want to skim over the slow-going parts, like working a job we don't enjoy. We want to skip painful life chapters, such as going through a divorce. And sometimes, we want to read ahead to discover how everything works out; for example, who our children will grow up to be.

Right now we are living in the middle of God's story. When the action is intense—your husband has been laid off and you don't know how you'll pay the bills; when the plot is heartbreaking—your dad has been diagnosed with a devastating illness; when the story line is exciting—God has called you to another place; in all of these things, we as Jesus followers know how the story ends. We've read ahead. We know the Author's good plan. And we can know that the characters in His story—us—are going to make it through to that happiest of all endings.

Jesus wins! He is coming again to restore all things (see Revelation 21:5), and we are on His winning team.

Rest Assured

Father, as we live in the middle of Your story, we've read ahead. We know that You have already won the victory, and we praise You.

Rest in Him: Revelation 21

words of reflection

A Healthy Sacrifice

I plead with you to give your bodies to God because of all he has done for you. Let them be a living and holy sacrifice—the kind he will find acceptable. This is truly the way to worship him.

ROMANS 12:1

Sarah observed her sister Tammy's journey to better health with interest and joy. She had long been concerned about Tammy's extra weight, stressful lifestyle, and minimal exercise. Even when Tammy's husband was diagnosed with diabetes, she hadn't altered her poor habits. And Tammy hadn't responded well when Sarah expressed her worries about the consequences of neglecting her health. Sarah had finally determined to stop fretting and began praying for God to work in Tammy's heart.

It wasn't long before Tammy finally decided to pursue healthy changes. Over a two-year period, she began exercising regularly and eating a more balanced diet. As her size changed and her health improved, so did her temperament. She smiled more often and took a greater interest in her relationships. Sarah continued to pray and cheered her on.

One day Tammy confided to Sarah, "God finally got my attention by reminding me that the way I treated my body was one reflection of my commitment to Him. He expects me to be a living sacrifice, holy and pleasing. I wanted that too. It hasn't been easy to break my bad habits. But making that surrender has changed my life."

Sarah smiled and breathed a prayer of thanksgiving that God had answered her.

The Bible is full of verses regarding the need for self-control in our lives. Developing that discipline is one of the keys to presenting our bodies as a living sacrifice. God is our power source, and His strength truly can work best in our weaknesses (see 2 Corinthians 12:9), whether we struggle with poor eating habits, a lack of exercise, or working too much and resting too little. But we must be willing to give Him control when we struggle. If you have health issues that need to be addressed, offer yourself to Him as a "living and holy sacrifice."

Rest Assured

Father, thank You that You are able to help us overcome our weaknesses. Show us where we are weak, and give us Your strength to make choices that are right and acceptable. We want to be holy and pleasing to You.

Rest in Him: 1 Corinthians 3:16-17

words of reflection

Sight Unseen

We don't look at the troubles we can see now; rather, we fix our gaze on things that cannot be seen. For the things we see now will soon be gone, but the things we cannot see will last forever.

2 CORINTHIANS 4:18

Recently, it seemed that Angie's life was being thrown into chaos—her fiancé lost his accounting job, there were managerial shake-ups at her workplace, her parents were in a car accident, and now her "check engine" light had come on.

As the engine light glowed, Angie squelched her anxious thoughts of *What else could happen?* She knew all too well that more could happen—both good and bad.

So she did the only thing she could do in rush hour traffic—turn off the music and pray. *Lord, this morning, I asked for help and direction, and now my check engine light has come on. I feel really overwhelmed right now. Please be merciful as I place my trust in You. You are my strength.*

Angie continued her prayer as she drove into the car repair shop. The mechanic looked over the car and suggested that she leave it overnight. While waiting to be picked up, Angie was surprised to hear herself telling the mechanic about the storm that seemed to be swirling around her. He perked up and told her that the mechanic shop was looking for a book-keeper and office manager. Hopeful, Angie asked for a job description and contact information. She knew that a job for her fiancé wouldn't tie up everything in a nice little bow, but she took it as a sign that God was working, even when she didn't clearly see all the details.

Sometimes when life gets overwhelming, we focus on fixing the problems. But what if we stopped in the middle of the storm and asked God to open our spiritual eyes? What if an engine light leads you to someone who has an answer to your problem or who needs a word of encouragement? We can ask God to show us how He's working in the midst of our circumstances. Then we can serve others better, respond more peacefully, and trust more deeply.

Rest Assured

Father, attune my heart and spiritual eyes to the unseen things You are doing. Give me discernment, and open the eyes of my heart as I seek to serve You.

Rest in Him: Ephesians 1:15-23

words of reflection

Joy in My Soul

The hope of the righteous is joy.
PROVERBS 10:28, HCSB

As a brand-new Christian in college, I was a member of an a cappella group. One of my favorite songs was a southern gospel–style quartet called "Feeling Mighty Fine." The opening lyrics, toe-tappingly upbeat, are "I woke up this morning feeling fine. I woke up with heaven on my mind. I woke up with joy in my soul, 'cause I knew my Lord had control."

Though I loved that song, for most of my life I struggled with the joy concept. After becoming a Christian, I thought maybe something was wrong with my faith. I thought I was supposed to be so visibly joyful that non-Christians couldn't help but notice and ask the reason for my joy. Then I would share Jesus on the spot, bringing another precious lamb into the fold.

After walking many years with Jesus, I still love that song, and I have learned two things about joy. One, it isn't something I can force. As a fruit of the Spirit, it is a natural result of remaining connected to the Vine. And two, joy is more about where I put my hope than about feelings. Just as the song says, when I remember and meditate on what I have to look forward to after this life—God restoring me and all of creation to perfection, no more tears, and no death to fear—that's joy.

You are not letting Jesus down if you're not the type of Christian who always has a smile on her face and a bounce in her step. Joy is about living in the truth that "the sufferings of this present time are not worth comparing with the glory that is going to be revealed to us" (Romans 8:18, HCSB). Believers can be joyful even through difficult seasons. We can have hopeful anticipation in the future because of the righteous standing God has given us, and He is faithful to His promises.

Rest Assured

Lord, help me to remember the imperishable, uncorrupted, and unfading inheritance I have in Christ, and let that hope fill me with Your joy.

Rest in Him: Galatians 5:16-25

words of reflection

Just Listen

The wisdom from above is first of all pure. It is also peace loving,
gentle at all times, and willing to yield to others. It is full of mercy
and the fruit of good deeds. It shows no favoritism
and is always sincere.

JAMES 3:17

"Abby really appreciated your support last week," Kate said as we walked into church.

I recalled my last conversation with Abby. Several of us had been having lunch when she shared about the conflict with her ex-husband that was taking the fun out of her daughter's wedding plans.

"I don't remember saying anything profound." All I had done was listen and assure Abby that I would be upset in her situation too.

"Nobody else but you noticed how upset she was. Abby told me that having you there, so sweet and sympathetic, kept her from bursting into tears."

At the time I was new in town and too shy to do anything but listen. This was one of my most powerful lessons in the impact of listening without judging, making light of the situation, or giving unsolicited advice. More than a decade later, I found myself listening to another friend as she unloaded an overwhelming difficulty in her life. Instead of wishing I had more to offer, I thanked God for the privilege of quietly sharing her burden.

"Thank you for being a safe friend," she said as we hugged good-bye.

I prayed that I would continue to be, both for her and for others.

Whom do you call when you need to talk? Do you run to the friend who responded to your last crisis by telling you to toughen up and trust God, or the gentle sister who sat at your side as you poured out your heart? Friends who reflect Christ's spirit of gentleness provide a safe haven for honesty and raw emotion, reminding us why Scripture calls us to be kind rather than harsh or cold. Memories of friends who took our late-night phone calls, shared our tears, and set their opinions aside and let us unload show us how to respond when someone else needs support.

Rest Assured

Lord, I want to be a friend that others know they can call on in a crisis or share their hearts with. Show me what I need to change in order to be a safe friend.

Rest in Him: Galatians 5:22-23

words of reflection

Running on Empty?

*Anyone who believes in me may come and drink! For the Scriptures
declare, "Rivers of living water will flow from his heart."*
JOHN 7:38

Sharon sat on the park bench looking out at the water. She had
packed a sack lunch to avoid her coworkers' usual invitations
to join them in the cafeteria. At the pace her life had recently
taken, Sharon needed time alone with God to reflect and refuel.

Unwrapping her sandwich and breathing in the mild
summer breeze, Sharon thanked God for giving her strength
to handle the extra responsibilities she had recently acquired
due to her mother's surgery. Not only did she have to care
for her family, balance work, and get her mother settled in an
assisted living center, but she would also need to tend to her
mother's plants, pets, and bills while she recuperated.

Father, Sharon prayed, *I read in Psalm 1 that if I meditate
on Your truths, You will make me like the trees planted by this
river. Even in the stressful times, I can flourish.* Sharon paused
to look at the tall, strong trees lining the bank of the river.
She listened to their leaves rustling in the wind and to the
sounds of the birds perched in their limbs.

A lot of people seem to need me right now, Sharon continued, *and that's a little daunting. But I know I can serve them well if You strengthen me. I'm really counting on You.*

While it's true that seasons come and go, some seasons of life are decidedly more stressful than others. When we encounter especially daunting circumstances, we may be tempted to dig a hole and hide or at least whine in self-pity. But the Bible teaches that we can accomplish all God calls us to do if we depend on Him to supply the nourishment our souls need for the task.

Psalm 42:5 reminds us to hope in the Lord when we are distressed; His presence will restore our praises. If you are going through a stressful season, make time to seek God. Allow Him to fill your soul so you can pour yourself out without resentment or reservation.

Rest Assured

Father, fill my soul with living water so I can pour freely into those around me.

Rest in Him: Isaiah 55:10-11

words of reflection

DAY 22

Building
Endurance

*We can rejoice, too, when we run into problems and trials,
for we know that they help us develop endurance.*
ROMANS 5:3

Everything was falling apart. So why wasn't I?

A few years earlier I had been drowning in depression and anxiety, reduced to tears by the smallest thing. How would I ever deal with a major life crisis if I couldn't even hold myself together through everyday misunderstandings or disappointments? As I grew stronger, however, I sensed God challenging me to trust Him. If He allowed a crisis, it would be because He knew I was strong enough for it. And amazingly, I experienced many and survived! Trials increased in intensity, gradually strengthening my faith, including my faith in His ability to keep me strong no matter what came my way.

But in this current situation, peace seemed almost unnatural considering the hugeness of what was going on. Was I in denial or experiencing a peace that could come only from God and several years of seeing Him at work? Suddenly I understood what Philippians 4:7 says when it mentions how the peace of God surpasses all understanding (ESV). Yes, life was falling apart in ways that seemed beyond repair. I needed to prepare for the worst-case scenario, but I didn't need to give in to despair. As I'd seen firsthand so many times, God wouldn't allow anything unless He was prepared to ride it out with me, provide for me, and keep me strong through it.

It doesn't require much faith when every prayer is answered immediately, bills are paid ahead of schedule, and everyone we love is in perfect health and making the right choices. We experience growth spurts of faith not when life is going smoothly, but when it's so out of control that only God can fix it.

God's Word provides answers not for *if* we face trials, but for *when* we face them. He also promises to use each trial, from daily disappointments to heart-shattering losses, to increase our faith as we seek and obey Him. Reflect on how past tests have prepared you for any current crises.

Rest Assured

Thank You, Father, for never wasting a crisis, but for using each one to deepen my relationship with You and strengthen my ability to trust Your plan.

Rest in Him: Romans 5:1-5

words of reflection

Standing Up and Sticking Out

If someone asks about your hope as a believer,
always be ready to explain it.

1 PETER 3:15

Grace Ann was a freshman in college when she took Philosophy 101, a huge lecture class. When the professor taught on relativism—the belief that truth is relative to each individual and cannot be fully known—Grace Ann felt compelled to point out the holes in that argument. She asked the professor if he believed that relativism was true. When he said he did, she mentioned that if relativism says there is no absolute truth, its proponents can't even say that *it* is true.

The professor smirked and said he had heard that argument before. He told Grace Ann that she should start thinking for herself now that she was in college and not fall back on the beliefs she was raised on.

He then said he would be happy to put any other naive freshmen in their place. Grace Ann shrank down in her seat, embarrassed and a little angry.

After class, several students thanked her for taking a stand. Even students who didn't agree with her said they admired the fact that she stood up for what she believed. The rest of the semester, Grace Ann continued to feel like the professor singled her out, so she always tried to be prepared for class and make comments that were respectful yet pointed toward a godly worldview. She stuck with the class and got a decent grade despite her professor's obvious dislike of her. But the greater reward was that she was faithful to the Lord and His Word.

God uses even the smallest daily acts of courage to build up His people, share His glory, and grow His Kingdom. Defending the weak, befriending the lonely, healing the broken, sharing the gospel, proclaiming the truth—those are the things Jesus spent His earthly ministry doing. And those things require great courage from us as we live in a way that shows what we truly believe.

Rest Assured

Lord, give me courage and confidence to speak the truth in Your mighty name and to trust You with the results.

Rest in Him: 2 Corinthians 4:16-18

words of reflection

Talking Away the Stress

You will keep in perfect peace all who trust in you,
all whose thoughts are fixed on you!
ISAIAH 26:3

I had plenty to do and a lot on my mind. I felt convinced that I wouldn't be able to focus until I got some peace. I called a friend whom I often prayed with, but we spent more time discussing problems than bringing all that was on our hearts to God. I poured out my frustrations in an e-mail to a Christian friend from work, and then when the phone rang, I seized the opportunity to rehash everything again. I set the phone down at almost 9:00 p.m. Instead of feeling more relaxed about my circumstances, I felt guilty for wasting so much time.

How often had I criticized other family members for turning to television, the computer, or sleep when life felt out of control? Like them, I was searching for a false source of peace. Instead of turning to a screen or a pillow, I turned to the phone and e-mail, chattering away hours and walking away just as discontent.

Now, with regret piled on top of what was already going

on, I felt even worse than when I started the day. *God, help me to make up the time*, I prayed silently. I began praying through everything that had driven me to the phone. The calm I longed for came, finally.

Lord, help me start here next time, and never let me forget the consequences of seeking comfort in the wrong places.

As believers, we know where true peace comes from, so why do we run so quickly to time wasters like the television, the computer, gadgets, or gossip? Isaiah's words remind us that God promises peace not to those who zone out in front of the television or who run around in a blur, but to those whose minds are steadfast. The assurance that comes after times of prayer can serve as a reminder of what we gain when we seek Him above all else.

Rest Assured

Lord, why do I expect to find peace in anything but You? Help me to run to You first, before anyone or anything else.

Rest in Him: Isaiah 26:3-7

words of reflection

True Delight

He will take delight in you with gladness. With his love, he will calm all your fears. He will rejoice over you with joyful songs.

ZEPHANIAH 3:17

My daughter Hannah came bouncing through the front door. "Hey, Mom! I'm grabbing my tennis bag and going to practice!"

"Hang on, hon. Just a reminder: You need to finish your last couple of college applications by this weekend. Also, don't forget you have an orchestra concert tomorrow night and the Habitat for Humanity build on Saturday."

"Mom, I know. I've got it all in my calendar on my phone!" she yelled as she ran upstairs.

Sometimes the push toward college seemed overwhelming. It dawned on me that as hard as I was working to help Hannah build up her college applications, this time with her at home was fleeting. I was forgetting where she was right now and how precious this time with her really was. I realized I was what one of the college reps referred to as a "helicopter parent."

I prayed, *God, instead of thinking of Hannah's life as a*

project, help me to enjoy her and to spend this time preparing her heart and soul for life as an adult, trusting that Your plan for her is best.

When Hannah came downstairs, I asked her to meet me for dinner after practice, just the two of us. I said we wouldn't talk college or schedules; we would just talk. Hannah was excited, and so was I.

The Bible says that God delights in us. We are His children, and He not only cares for us, but He also knows us deeply. We can model God's love to our children by spending time listening to them, entering into their interests, and sharing their joys and sorrows. Spend a few minutes today with your children and don't have any sort of agenda. Just do what they enjoy doing or talk about what's on their minds. Quality time will build your relationships and give your children a sense of your love and interest in who they are.

Rest Assured

God, thank You for intimately knowing and caring for me as Your child. Help me to freely show that love and care to others.

Rest in Him: 1 John 3:1-3

words of reflection

A Work of Art

*The LORD is like a father to his children, tender and compassionate
to those who fear him. For he knows how weak we are;
he remembers we are only dust.*

PSALM 103:13-14

After he retired, my grandfather took up painting. He was naturally talented, and a few of his pieces—a giant sunflower in oil, a watercolor rabbit—now hang in my home. When my brother and I were little, Grandpa took us out to his studio so we could create our own watercolors. We each held the paintbrush, but he guided our hands.

My brother's piece is quite good. It's a forest scene of rich greens and browns. My painting features a flower-dotted hill set against a bright blue sky with some high-floating clouds. But at some point when Grandpa wasn't watching, I took some white paint and dabbed it on the hill to make a river or stream. It looks all wrong—no stream starts and stops in the middle of a hill! What might have been a fairly polished watercolor was ruined (though my parents framed and displayed it anyway).

Have you ever tried to follow the Lord's will, only to sense that you have moved too far from His plan? Perhaps you wonder whether God can use you after your divorce, your betrayal, or your relapse into addiction. Just as I messed up a simple painting when I didn't let my grandpa guide me, perhaps you feel as if you've made such a mess of things that God can't redeem your situation.

We can take comfort in the way our heavenly Father continually woos His straying people throughout Scripture. King David killed a man to cover up his adultery; later he failed to act when one of his sons assaulted his own half sister. Yes, David paid a steep price in both cases, yet God never abandoned the one He called "a man after my own heart" (Acts 13:22).

Your Father hasn't given up on you either. Just ask, and He will take your hand in His and begin to restore your life.

Rest Assured

Father God, I confess that I blow it often. Remind me today that You are the ultimate Redeemer—and You are not finished with me yet.

Rest in Him: Hosea 14

words of reflection

Never Too Busy

The eyes of the LORD search the whole earth in order to strengthen those whose hearts are fully committed to him.

2 CHRONICLES 16:9

My dad was a high school English teacher. Most weeknights, after dinner was over and the dishes were done, he would grade papers in his "home office"—a metal desk and a filing cabinet at the bottom of the stairs of our unfinished basement. I would often head down the stairs myself in the evenings to sharpen a pencil, to search for my cat, Cricket—or simply to talk to my dad.

I can't remember a single conversation we had, but I do remember this: No matter how high the stack of essays he needed to grade, Dad would always stop what he was doing when he heard me clomping down those stairs. I can still picture him, wrapped in an afghan or wearing his jacket to ward off the basement chill, putting down his pen and turning toward me when he saw me hit that bottom step. He was never too busy for me.

Without preaching and without my knowing it, my dad was showing me what our heavenly Father is like—always searching for the one who seeks Him out. He longs to spend time with His children, and He is never preoccupied or too busy with more important stuff to listen to us.

I have a wonderful dad, but he is not infallible. God the Father, however, is perfect—perfectly loving, perfectly powerful, and perfectly wise. Do you need direction? Ask Him for guidance. Do you wonder if you matter? Seek Him out. Do you struggle with fear? Cry out to Him.

Your heavenly Father is near you, and He is just waiting to hear your voice and respond to your need.

Rest Assured

Abba Father, how thankful I am to know that I can come to You anytime. No matter how unworthy or lost I feel, You are waiting to fill me with Your presence, peace, and love.

Rest in Him: Isaiah 30:15-21

words of reflection

The Rewards
of the Risk

*Now do as I tell you. . . . Be sure to notice where [Boaz] lies down;
then go and uncover his feet and lie down there.*

RUTH 3:3-4

I've always loved the biblical character Ruth. She risked going
to a foreign land to live, where the only person she knew
was Naomi, her *mother-in-law*. She risked finding work in
a stranger's field. She risked obeying her mother-in-law's
request to lie down at the feet of a man and ask him to marry
her and care for her. That's seriously scandalous!

I would have balked if my mother-in-law—or anyone!—
told me to make such a request. I'd feel as if I were reliving my
freshman year, in which I told a senior that I had a crush on
him—to which he replied awkwardly, "Uh, thanks," and then
avoided me like the plague for the rest of his high school career.

Never again. Better to play it safe, and no one will think
you're crazy.

But Ruth trusted Naomi and took the risk. And did it
ever pay off! God used her willingness to step outside her
comfort zone to accomplish His will—not only in her life
but in the life of an entire nation.

Imagine, had she not trusted God and Naomi, she might not have married Boaz or had a baby (Obed), who would never have married and had a baby (Jesse), who would have never had a son, David—the David who became the famous king of Jewish history and acclaim, and who was the ancestor of our Savior, Jesus. So much history set in place—all because Ruth took a risk.

Is there something you feel God calling you to do, but fear keeps you from pursuing it? Perhaps today is the day to say yes to the risk—and the potential reward.

Rest Assured

Jesus, You came to earth through the lineage of a woman who moved beyond her fears and said yes to scary and crazy things—things well out of her comfort zone. I want to have that kind of willingness and faith to trust You even when I don't know the outcome that You have planned.

Rest in Him: Ruth 3:1-13

words of reflection

Fix Your Thoughts

Fix your thoughts on what is true, and honorable, and right, and pure, and lovely, and admirable. Think about things that are excellent and worthy of praise.

PHILIPPIANS 4:8

I smiled as I watched my three-year-old granddaughter sleeping peacefully. Madison didn't have a care in the world. Happy, healthy, and well loved, her biggest concern was whether she would receive the new doll she had been asking for. I wished I could experience the peace she had.

Instead I was filled with so much worry and anxiety that it was disrupting my sleep. My son-in-law was battling metastatic melanoma, and we didn't know what the outcome would be. As a result, our oldest daughter was shouldering a huge burden of stress. Our youngest daughter faced severe financial problems, and her husband's company had just announced layoffs. My mother had married a man who was isolating her from the rest of the family, which made maintaining a relationship with her difficult. And my own mental health was deteriorating.

Night after night, I could feel the anxiety churning inside. I tried not to get up too often so I wouldn't disturb my husband, but he wasn't sleeping very well either.

One night we were both awake about 2:00 a.m., so I turned on the light and picked up my Bible. It fell open to the verse in Philippians that says, "Fix your thoughts on what is . . . pure, and lovely" (4:8). We prayed that the Lord would give us peace while we went through life's storms and that He would help us to focus on Him and His faithfulness.

When we're overwhelmed with our circumstances, it's hard to focus on the pure and lovely things in our lives. The Lord wants us to face our concerns and give them to Him. Because of Jesus, we no longer have to let our burdens consume us. The next time you're tempted to fret, pause, take a deep breath, and picture giving your burdens to the Lord. He is more than able to carry you through.

Rest Assured

Lord, You are good, and Your love is eternal. Your faithfulness continues to all generations (see Psalm 100:5).

Rest in Him: Philippians 4:4-9

words of reflection

How God Views Us

*The LORD doesn't see things the way you see them. People judge by
outward appearance, but the LORD looks at the heart.*

1 SAMUEL 16:7

The dog was the ugliest thing I'd ever seen. Sometimes "ugly"
is so ugly it's actually cute. Not in this case. This dog had
matted, thinning hair over most of his back. The rest of him
was bald. He had milky-white eyes, giving away his blind-
ness. His lower jaw had a large underbite, revealing three dis-
colored teeth. His breath could have taken out enemy forces.

When I first saw him, all I could utter was "Oh my. Bless
his heart."

His owner chuckled at my shock as she picked up her dog
and cuddled against him. "They were going to put him down
at the shelter because nobody wanted to give him a chance.
Everyone thought he wasn't valuable because of the way he
looks. But this dog saved my life when I was going through
depression. He accepted and loved me unconditionally. To
me, he's priceless and beautiful."

As I watched this owner lavish affection on her pet, I
stood amazed by how God often hides special gifts in plain

wrapping paper. Too often we view the outward appearance and judge a person's—and our own!—abilities based on looks. God doesn't necessarily choose the most beautiful and perfectly urbane, refined, chic people to have the greatest gifts.

What freedom! When I look in the mirror and see someone "less than," I have the assurance that God sees the inner self and says, *To Me, she has value and purpose. She's priceless and beautiful.*

Thank God that He uses us no matter how we look! He doesn't expect us to be "prettied up" before He puts us to work in His Kingdom. We don't have to lose those thirty pounds first, or get the nose job, or have the right hairstyle, or clean ourselves up on the inside. God bless that ugly dog for using the gifts His Creator placed within him—it's a good dose of real beauty and humility.

Rest Assured

Father, sometimes I can get so caught up in falsely feeling "less than" in my appearance that I think You would never use me. Forgive me for believing that lie. Use me today—just as I am. Thank You.

Rest in Him: 1 Peter 3:3-4; 1 Samuel 16:1-13

words of reflection

Don't Melt

*God blessed the seventh day and declared it holy, because it was
the day when he rested from all his work of creation.*

GENESIS 2:3

The snow fell in thick, silent flakes one Friday night as I
returned home from dinner with friends. As I left to run
errands the next morning, I watched two neighbor kids roll-
ing snowballs nearly as big as they were.

When I arrived home a few hours later, I couldn't miss the
finished snowman, glistening in the sunlight near the edge of
our yards. He was a stocky fellow with rocks for eyes, a carrot
for a nose, and a curved stick for a mouth. A purple scarf was
tied jauntily around his neck.

After cleaning the kitchen, I left for the grocery store.
Pulling out of the driveway, I noticed that the snowman was
leaning and shrinking a bit. Uh-oh. Sure enough, by the time
I returned home after attending church and sneaking in a few
hours of work Sunday afternoon, all that was left of Frosty
were some piles of snow and the purple scarf. By Monday
morning, the scarf was gone and just a few small mounds of
snow remained on the lawn.

Frankly, I felt a bit like that snowman: totally spent. Its short life span—Saturday morning to early Monday morning—reminded me of the state of my soul just then. The hours and minutes that seemed to stretch out on Friday began to melt away as the weekend wore on. I may have checked off the boxes on my to-do list, but I was exhausted by the time a new workweek rolled around.

My tendency is to cram in as many errands, outings, and chores as I can on a weekend. After all, how else will I get everything done? I'm old enough to know, however, that my body simply can't take that pace. When I ignore reality, I pay on Monday. On the other hand, when I obey God by observing the Sabbath—by "keeping it holy" (Exodus 20:8)—I am filled up rather than depleted. God knew that we needed the Sabbath as a time to connect deeply with Him and other believers, as well as a time to rest.

Just as that snowman wasn't made for sun, we weren't built for nonstop activity. We may not be able to do much about the weather, but we can choose to slow our pace.

Rest Assured

Lord God, thank You for loving me enough to create the Sabbath. May I take that time this week to rest my body and allow You to restore my soul.

Rest in Him: Isaiah 58:13-14

words of reflection

The Reason for Our Joy

Yes, the LORD has done amazing things for us! What joy!

PSALM 126:3

I took my favorite picture of my son when he was about four. He'd been spinning in circles as he ran around my parents' big backyard. In the photo, he is laughing and his arms are raised high. Both his body and his face express one emotion: pure joy.

No wonder I think of this picture when I read the opening verses of Psalm 126, which celebrate the Israelites' return from Babylonian exile. God had fulfilled His promise to bring His people home, and they couldn't stop singing, laughing, and telling others about His goodness. I even imagine them pinching themselves when the psalmist says their return was "like a dream!" (verse 1). Exuberance was on full display—just as it's written all over my son's face in that photo.

God pours His grace on us every day, giving us many reasons to rejoice. Of course, we still live in a broken world, and the psalmist acknowledges that, too. My son has faced many difficulties since that sunny day when he was four, and it's clear from the later books of the Old Testament that the Israelites faced challenges when they returned to their land. Perhaps that is why the psalmist also talks of weeping and planting "in tears" (verse 5) as he calls on the Lord to "restore our fortunes" (verse 4).

In this life, we treasure moments of pure joy in part because they are so fleeting. Yet embracing and capturing those glimpses of God's goodness—whether in our minds' eye or in our photo albums—leaves imprints of hope in our hearts. God's loving-kindness has become real to us, so even when difficulty creeps back into our lives, we know we can "harvest with shouts of joy" (verse 5).

So if you see the Lord working in an amazing way today, celebrate! And if the day brings trouble instead, remember that God will bless you as you faithfully follow His leading. He is at work redeeming and restoring your life, even as you wait for the day when He guides you all the way home.

Rest Assured

Heavenly Father, thank You that joy is a hallmark of Your Kingdom. Whether or not my circumstances give me reason to be joyful today, help me to celebrate Your goodness and to wait with hope.

Rest in Him: Romans 15:13

words of reflection

The Perfect Planner

I trust in you, LORD; I say, "You are my God."
My times are in your hands.

PSALM 31:14-15, NIV

At the end of every year my favorite aisle in the bookstore is the one stacked high with planners, which are always placed just below the racks of wall calendars. There is an organizer for everyone: students, moms, professionals, and athletes. Some feature weekly or daily spreads; others show a month at a time. I'm always drawn first to the ones with the artsy colorful covers. When I pick up one of those, I imagine how inspired I'd be by its beautiful design.

In the end, though, I always end up buying the newest edition of the same spiral-bound weekly planner because I like its layout best. I can block out meetings in a way that gives me a visual overview of how much uninterrupted work time I have each day. There is also plenty of room to take notes.

Still, every year I search for that perfect planner that will help me not only organize my schedule but perfect it. Maybe, I think, someone has invented a tool that will help me overcome all my bad habits while faithfully working in the good ones. Maybe I'll stumble across a planner that will magically reveal time in my day that I never knew I had—or at least help me organize my days so well that I'll be able to fit even more into my schedule.

Deep inside, I know that ideal planner doesn't exist. And I'm okay with that. God didn't create you and me to be automatons who never stop working or never relax and enjoy our families. He created stars to mark the passage of seasons and years, and He made a world that operates within the limits of time.

Planners, digital or paper, are wonderful tools that can help us steward the coming year well. They can remind us of our obligations and our priorities. However, they will never enable us to run the universe. Thankfully, that job is already taken: Our Lord Jesus "existed before anything else, and he holds all creation together" (Colossians 1:17).

That's good news we can plan on and rest in every day in the year ahead!

Rest Assured

Lord Jesus, I commit this coming year to You, knowing that You go ahead of me and will cover me with Your mercy and grace.

Rest in Him: Proverbs 16:1-9

words of reflection

Take Time for You

Whatever you do, do it enthusiastically, as something done for the Lord and not for men.

COLOSSIANS 3:23, HCSB

"See you tomorrow!" I called as my coworker walked into the elevator. Once again, I was the last one to leave the office. The hours I stayed late or came in early were quiet and calm, so I could actually get work done without being overtaken with meetings. I pulled out a bag of chips from my desk and settled in for another two or three hours of work. On my drive home at 10:00 p.m., I called my best friend, Kim, to catch up.

"Hey," she answered, flatly.

"Hey," I said. "You okay?"

"Tonight was Kristi's going-away party; she leaves for Kenya tomorrow."

My heart dropped. I'd forgotten about the party for my cousin who'd answered God's call to serve in Kenya for a year.

For the remainder of the drive home, Kim spoke boldly to me about the dangers of letting my career consume me. "Overworking is taking a toll on your health and on your relationships," she said.

It was true. Lately, it felt like I practically lived at the office. So I asked Kim for help. We set up a daily phone call at 6:30 p.m. so that we could read a passage from the Bible and pray together. The timing would allow me to get home, get comfortable, and meet with Kim on the phone.

Soon, I began to see the benefits of having balance, and I arranged my schedule to allow for more God time.

Has work gotten so large in your life that it's starting to affect your relationships and your health? Scripture tells us to work for the Lord and not people—not your boss, but not yourself either. Work for the Lord, period. Burning yourself out and alienating others do not indicate a career given to the Lord. Set boundaries, include time for yourself and for serving others, and begin to gain a healthy balance.

Rest Assured

Father, help me spend my time wisely and responsibly. Provide opportunities for me to rest and serve others.

Rest in Him: Matthew 6:19-21

words of reflection

Take Time to Listen

My sheep listen to my voice;
I know them, and they follow me.
JOHN 10:27

Over steaming cups of tea, Jan and I got caught up on our news. Then I asked this question: "I tell God all my requests, but sometimes I wonder if He's really there. I mean, how do you know He is? It's not like He says anything back."

Jan answered, "Good question. You said that you tell God your requests. Do you do any listening?"

"Listening? Hmmm. Well . . . no, I guess not."

"I'm just starting to understand its importance in prayer. I used to talk the whole time."

"But isn't that what we're supposed to do? Otherwise, we'd just be sitting there, right?"

"Prayer is, at its heart, a conversation. We praise and thank God and share our requests with Him. But we're also supposed to listen. To be quiet and let Him speak."

"Out loud?"

"Well, not usually, but in your heart and mind. It helps to be actively listening. Read a passage from His Word and let it soak in as you sit. Ask Him to show you what He wants you to see in it and how to apply it to your life."

"Okay, I'll try that, though I'm not always good at sitting still."

"Me neither! But we can't expect to hear God if we're doing all the talking. When we are quiet and wait on Him, we are in a better position to hear from Him."

We encourage children to sit and be quiet, but sometimes we don't give ourselves the time to do the same. In order to hear the voice of God, we need to allow Him space and time in our lives to speak. Meditating on Scripture—letting it percolate in our hearts—can quiet us and help us focus. The Bible shows God speaking in different ways. Don't miss His voice, however it comes to you.

Rest Assured

Father, help me be quiet and listen. Open my heart to hear Your voice.

Rest in Him: 1 Kings 19:1-18

words of reflection

God's Grace in the Clouds

You live under the freedom of God's grace.
ROMANS 6:14

Lately, I've taken a profound interest in clouds. Puffy, fluffy, billowy white clouds or cottony swishes splashed across the sky that reflect brilliant sunbeams behind and around them. And at dusk—oh my!—the colors are magnificent. Magentas, ambers, baby blues, burgundies, silvers. It's as if the angels grabbed a box of Crayolas and decorated the heavens. Almost every evening, I walk outside, and like a five-year-old, I identify flying dragons and dogs wearing party hats.

What's most wonderful about the clouds, though, is that every day they are brand-new. There are always new shapes and colors for me to enjoy and appreciate (even the gray, dull, dreary ones). Don't like today's clouds? No problem. Tomorrow will offer a plethora of new choices. No need even to wait for tomorrow. Just wait a few minutes, and the sky will change.

Looking at clouds reminds us that God isn't a God of second chances. Woe to us if He were. God is a God of *infinite* chances. Just as those clouds change and re-form over and over, God's grace toward us is new every day, every minute.

When we need grace, we don't have to wait minutes or days for it to materialize. We have grace available to us right then—when we humbly ask for it.

I'm not sure I'll ever look at clouds without a renewed sense of hope. They point to a God who loves to creatively pour out grace on us whenever we need it, whose faithfulness to us is as certain as the sky.

Rest Assured

God, everywhere I look, I see Your creativity and the newness You offer. Even the sky shows that You bring renewed hope and grace to me. Help me look up as often as I can.

Rest in Him: Psalm 36:5-10

words of reflection

Find Us Faithful

A faithful [woman] will have many blessings.
PROVERBS 28:20, HCSB

Several years ago, I became interested in using dogs for therapy work, so I contacted a therapy group in my area and took the necessary steps to train my Doberman pinscher. After he passed his tests, Diesel and I were ready to go.

I made a commitment to visit a local nursing home twice a month. Every other week, I bathed and groomed Diesel. Then I tied a bandanna around his neck and loaded him into my SUV for the trip to the nursing home. The residents looked forward to our visits, and Diesel loved the extra attention.

Sometimes I was tempted to sleep in on Saturday mornings. As a busy working woman, I didn't always feel like getting up early and going through the routine of bathing and grooming Diesel. But I had made a commitment, and I thought it was important to keep it.

We developed a special relationship with an eighty-five-year-old widow. Mrs. Tate stroked Diesel's sleek black coat while she told stories about her husband, who had served in

World War II, and her children and grandchildren, who lived in other states.

One Saturday as Diesel rested his head in Mrs. Tate's lap, I began to tell her about the love of Jesus. While she had always had a basic belief in God, she didn't have a personal relationship with Him. During each visit, I told her how God was working in my life and that He wanted a special relationship with her, too.

After several weeks of my witnessing to Mrs. Tate, she embraced Jesus as her Savior. Two weeks later when Diesel and I visited the nursing home, her bed was empty. She had gone home to be with the Lord. I'm thankful that God helped me to be faithful to my commitment.

If you feel the Lord is leading you to make a commitment to something or someone, ask Him to provide you with the grace and strength you'll need to follow through. Don't let schedules or the little details of your life derail God's plan for you. If He has called you to do something, He will bless you for being obedient.

Rest Assured

Father, thank You for being interested in the details of my life. Please help me to be faithful to the commitments You have called me to make so that others will give glory to You.

Rest in Him: Psalm 18:24-27

words of reflection

God's Currency

What is the price of two sparrows—one copper coin?
But not a single sparrow can fall to the ground without your Father
knowing it. . . . So don't be afraid; you are more valuable
to God than a whole flock of sparrows.

MATTHEW 10:29, 31

When I was a child, finding a penny on the ground made my day. With it, I could buy a gum ball at the grocery store, or if I collected ten, I could afford one of the bouncy rubber balls from the dispenser next to the gum ball machine.

Not long ago, however, I walked right by a penny in a parking lot. In a nanosecond, I decided that stooping to pick it up wasn't worth the effort. After all, about the only time I use pennies now is when trying to give exact change to a cashier so I can avoid getting more of them!

Interestingly, Jesus found great value in pennies (okay, the copper coins of His day) as a teaching tool. When talking with His disciples about the troubles to come, He urged them not to worry. After all, God was aware of every sparrow, each of which was worth less than one copper coin. He added, "The very hairs on your head are all numbered. So don't be afraid" (Matthew 10:30-31). Only our awesome almighty God, who controls world events and establishes leaders (see Daniel 2:21), is big and powerful enough to track the tiniest details in our lives.

Later, Jesus watched wealthy worshipers dropping gifts in the Temple collection box. Along came a poor widow, who dropped in two small copper coins. Why did He commend this woman? "They have given a tiny part of their surplus, but she, poor as she is, has given everything she has" (Luke 21:4). Only our compassionate Creator, who loves us and longs for our love in return, prizes the smallest sacrifices offered with the greatest love.

In God's economy, the seemingly small and insignificant never go unnoticed. If you feel forgotten today, remember that Christ sees you and will provide all that you need. If you wonder whether your contribution—of time, talents, or treasure—is too small to make a difference, remember that God evaluates each offering, not on its size, but on the heart from which it is given.

Rest Assured

Lord, thank You for assigning worth even to those things that the wider world views as insignificant. Help me to rest in Your watchful care and to give generously from a grateful heart.

Rest in Him: 2 Corinthians 8:1-5

words of reflection

DAY 39

Help Is Coming

Your God is coming. . . . He is coming to save you.
ISAIAH 35:4

Black smoke billowed from the burning car as April helped the driver to a safe distance. "Help is coming," she promised as the driver coughed and struggled to breathe. With the car now engulfed in flames, there was nothing to do but keep giving first aid and wait for the first responders to arrive.

In a lull in her conversation with the 911 dispatcher, April repeated her assurance to the driver in distress: "Help is coming."

Those three simple words, April would later contemplate, can make all the difference in the world. They offer the promise that we are not alone, that our predicament is seen and recognized, and that someone qualified to rescue us has taken notice of our plight and is on the way to do something about it.

The promise of help and rescue has inspired hope through the centuries, but it was never more needed than for the Jewish people over 2,500 years ago. The country had split into two separate kingdoms; one of them was on the verge of being destroyed, and the other didn't have a much brighter future. Things were looking grim, and God's prophets, the men and women He spoke through, were foretelling destruction and death.

But help was coming. Speaking on behalf of the Lord, the prophet Isaiah said, "That time of darkness and despair will not go on forever" (Isaiah 9:1). God was promising help in the form of a Messiah who would come on His behalf, saving Israel and the world. A child would be born, a Son given, and the Spirit of the Lord would rest on Him. God Himself would come down to earth and personally do the rescuing.

There was nothing to do but wait and hold on to the promise that the Messiah was coming. Over the next seven hundred years, the people of Israel anticipated His arrival. And then one night in the tiny village specified by the prophet Micah, the child was born. Now God was among humans, putting into motion His plan of hope and salvation.

Help had come.

Rest Assured

Thank You, God, for the hope Jesus' birth brings. Help us not take for granted the incredible gift we've been given.

Rest in Him: Isaiah 9:1-7

words of reflection

He Knows My Name

I have called you by name; you are mine.

ISAIAH 43:1

Did you know that scientists believe that at the center of every galaxy is a supermassive black hole, which holds the galaxy in place? I learned that on the Science Channel when they ran a program on what we know about the universe. At one point the TV screen swirled with all these multicolored, multishaped, multigaseous galaxies. When my eyes took them all in, I felt as if my brain exploded with the wonder of how awesomely vast and ordered our universe is—and how awesomely vast and ordered our *God* is.

Just looking at the photos from space of other planets—and even our own!—shows us the creativity and power of the Creator God. Whenever I drive through the mountains or stand on the beach and watch the force of the waves crashing against the sand, I find myself in awe of how immense God is. And I worship Him.

I worship the Creator God for His creativity and power, but I also worship Him because this great big, omnipotent, invincible God who created supermassive black holes to hold together galaxies knows my name. And He knows your name.

In the midst of a busy schedule—creating new worlds, overseeing the earth's entire population, handling the universe—He knows *your* name. Not only that, the God of the universe cares enough about you to number each hair that you have (see Luke 12:7). He knows every detail of your life. He calls you His.

So the next time you stand in awe at something in creation and are overwhelmed by how enormous and ordered and creative God is, you can rest in the knowledge that He's sovereign. He has everything under control, He knows you and what you need, and He's powerful enough to take care of those needs.

Rest Assured

Creator God, You know my name! You know who I am—my strengths, my vulnerabilities, my joys, my sorrows, my fears, my successes. And You care about them all. Thank You that every day through creation You show me that You're powerful enough to handle everything in my life.

Rest in Him: Psalm 8:3-4; Isaiah 51:12-13, 15-16

words of reflection

About Walk Thru the Bible

Walk Thru the Bible ignites passion for God's Word through innovative live events, inspiring biblical resources, and a global impact that changes lives worldwide . . . including yours.

Known for innovative methods and high-quality resources, we serve the whole body of Christ across denominational, cultural, and national lines. We partner with the local church worldwide to fulfill its mission, communicating the truths of God's Word in a way that makes the Bible readily accessible to anyone. Through our strong global network, we are strategically positioned to address the church's greatest need: developing mature, committed, and spiritually reproducing believers.

Our live events and small group curricula are taught in more than 50 languages by more than 80,000 people in more than 130 countries. More than 100 million devotionals have been packaged into daily magazines, books, and other publications that reach over five million people each year.

Wherever you are on your journey, we can help.

Walk Thru the Bible
www.walkthru.org
1.800.361.6131

Becoming the masterpiece God created you to be

In God's hands, anyone can become a masterpiece. In *Chiseled*, we'll study the life of Simon Peter and how God made him into the man, the leader, He always intended him to be. His work in Peter's life shows how He can work in our lives, too, to lovingly shape and sculpt us into the likeness of His Son—living masterpieces that will forever reflect the beauty and glory of the Artist Himself.

walkthru.org/chiseled

otLIVE is a catalyst for renewing your relationship with God and brings the Bible to life—helping you understand the BIG PICTURE of the Word of God in a FUN, ENGAGING, and LIFE-CHANGING way! At the *otLIVE* event, participants get out of their seats and on their feet as they learn through engaging hand signs, key words and phrases, and active participation.

The *otLIVE* Event:
- inspires people to read the Bible;
- increases understanding of Scripture's storyline;
- illustrates how the pieces of the Old Testament fit together;
- teaches the big picture of the Bible.